Trick or Treat

Silly Halloween Jokes

for Kids

Frank N. Stein

TABLE OF CONTENTS

Introduction 8

Instructions 10

Witch Jokes 11

Zombies Jokes 33

Vampire Jokes 57

Ghost Jokes 81

Halloween Jokes 104

Conclusion 126

© COPYRIGHT 2020 KONNECTD KIDS - ALL RIGHTS RESERVED.

The content contained within this book may not be reproduced, duplicated or transmitted without direct written permission from the author or the publisher.

Under no circumstances will any blame or legal responsibility be held against the publisher, or author, for any damages, reparation, or monetary loss due to the information contained within this book. Either directly or indirectly.

Legal Notice:

This book is copyright protected. This book is only for personal use. You cannot amend, distribute, sell, use, quote or paraphrase any part, or the content within this book, without the consent of the author or publisher.

Disclaimer Notice:

Please note the information contained within this document is for educational and entertainment purposes only. All effort has been executed to present accurate, up to date, and reliable, complete information. No warranties of any kind are declared or implied. Readers acknowledge that the author is not engaging in the rendering of legal, financial, medical or professional advice. The content within this book has been derived from various sources. Please consult a licensed professional before attempting any techniques outlined in this book.

By reading this document, the reader agrees that under no circumstances is the author responsible for any losses, direct or indirect, which are incurred as a result of the use of the information contained within this document, including, but not limited to, — errors, omissions, or inaccuracies.

KONNECTD KIDS
c/- Supply Mechanix LLC
30 N Gould St STE R
Sheridan, Wyoming, 82801
United States of America

www.konnectdkids.com
www.konnectdsupply.com
beawesome@konnectdkids.com
Facebook.com/konnectdkids
Instagram.com/konnectdkids

SPECIAL BONUS!

Get this Halloween Coloring Book 100% FREE!

Hundreds of others are already enjoying insider access to current and future books, 100% free!

If you want insider access, plus this Halloween Coloring book, all you have to do is **scan the code below or put the link into your web browser** to claim your offer!

https://tinyurl.com/y5rqbqjm

Introduction

Are you ready for Halloween? Halloween is a fun time of the year and a great time to practice your trick or treating on your family and friends.

Trick or Treat: Silly Halloween Jokes for Kids, gives you a Spooktacular chance to have your family, friends and neighbours in fits of laughter as you deliver some of these silly Halloween jokes. You can also use this book to enjoy a fantastic game night filled with laughter and spooky moments by seeing if anyone can guess the answer to the joke, pun or would you rather challenge.

Included are some downright silly and unforgettable Jokes that will have you either giggling with laughter or groaning at how lame they are! Some of the amazeballs Halloween jokes are:

Q. Where does the vegetarian Ghost get his vegetables from?
A. At the Ghostery store!

Q. What music do Ghosts like to play?
A. Spiritual music!

This great book has the best trick or treat riddles, tricky tongue twisters, fang-tastic knock-knock jokes, and funny laugh out loud Witch, Vampire, Ghost, Zombie and all out silly Halloween jokes. We hope you enjoy this book and use it to make some Halloween magic with your family by creating the best Halloween memories!

Instructions

How you want to use this book of silly Halloween jokes is up to you. You can read them to your family or take it with you Trick or Treating around the neighbourhood to tell them to unsuspecting neighbours.

A good laugh is best shared, so one suggestion is that you can take turns with different players asking the questions and other family members giving their best shot at answering them. Whatever way you decide to use these jokes the most important thing is to have a fun and Happy Halloween!

Witch Jokes
Tricky Witchy jokes to make Halloween fun

TWitchy Puns

Q. What happened to the Witch when she got caught casting spells on her classmates?
A. She got ex-spelled from Witch school!

Q. What do you call two Witches sharing a broom?
A. Broom-mates!

Q. Why do Witches say they invented the alphabet?
A. Because they know how to do spells!

Q. Where do Witches store all their clothes?
A. A broom-closet!

Q. What is a Witch's favorite food?
A. Sand-Witch

Q. What do you call a Witch allergic to her broom?
　　A. Broom-sick

Q. What did the Witch say to the invisible man?
　　A. Long-time no see!

Q. What did the Witch ask the angry monkey?
　　A. Why are you going bananas?

Q. Which cream do Witches like?
　　A. Itch cream!

Q. What did the Witch's broom do when it felt tired?
A. It over-swept.

Q. What do Witches love to apply to their eyes?
A. Ma-scare-ra!

Q. How did the little Witch pass English?
A. She knew how to spell!

Q. Why did the Witch faint after soccer practice?
A. She had a dizzy spell!

Q. How do Witches keep their hats so pointy?
A. They use sharpeners!

Q. How are Witches and Wizards similar?
A. They both have pointy hats!

Q. What do you call a Witch who loves poison ivy?
A. Itchy Witchy!

Q. Why do Witches ride on brooms and not vacuum cleaners?
A. Because vacuum cleaners are too expensive!

Q. Why did the police officer arrest the Witch?
A. Because she didn't have a license to cast spells!

Q. Where do baby Witches stay during the day?
A. They go to Day-scare!

Q. If a Witch loses her broom, how does she get upstairs?
A. She uses the Scare-case!

Q. Which show do Witches like to watch on TV?
A. BeWitched Re-runs!

Q. What would you call a Witch who becomes a millionaire overnight?
A. Very, very Wrich!

Q. What did the Witch tell Dracula?
A. You really do suck!

Q. What did the Witch tell the Zombie?
A. Something smells rotten in here!

Q. What did the Witch tell the spirit?
A. I can't see you!

Q. What do little Witches do on their birthdays?
A. They spellebrate!

Q. What do you call a motorbike that Witches ride?
A. A barooooooom Stick!

Q. What has a pointy hat and nose and jumps up and down?
A. A Witch on a trampoline!

Q. Why did the Witch stop telling people their futures?
A. She saw no future in foretelling!

Q. What dessert do Witches eat for dinner?
A. I-scream!

Q. How did the little Witch get the shiny trophy?
A. She won the spelling bee!

Q. What sound do Witches' brooms make when ridden at high speed?
A. Broom, broom!

Q. Why was the Witch under the weather?
A. She had been casting cloudy spells all day long!

Q. How do you confuse a Witch?
A. Mess up her spelling!

Q. Where do Witches keep their money?
A. In their hag bags!

Q. Why did the Witch drive to work?
A. Because her broom was not working!

Q. Is it bad to see a Witch's cat?
A. No, but if you're a mouse, you need to start running!

Q. Why was the little Witch sad about her test results?
A. Because she failed spelling!

Q. What's a Witch's favorite meal?
A. Green frogs!

Q. Why did the Witch like little children?
A. Because they tasted great!

Q. What do you call a Witch on Instagram?
A. Witch and famous!

Q. What do you call an anxious Witch?
A. TWitch

Q. What did the Witch tell the kid waiting at the door?
A. BeWitcha in a minute!

Q. What classes do artsy Witches take?
A. Arts and Witchcrafts!

Q. What do you call a Witch who wishes a lot?
A. Witch-ful thinker!

Knock-knock jokes

Knock knock.
Who's there
Wanda.
Wanda who?
Wanda ride my broom to Transylvania!

Knock knock.
Who's there?
Gargoyle
Gargoyle who?
Gargoyle the Witch's syrup if you want to get rid of the tummy ache.

Knock knock.
Who's there?
Witches!
Witches who?
Witches the way to the haunted forest?

Knock knock.
Who's there?
Figs!
Figs who?
Figs the broom, it's not working!

Knock knock.
Who's there?
Annie!
Annie who?
Annie thing the big Witch can do, I can do it too!

Knock knock.
Who's there?
Hal!
Hal who?
Hal will you see the Witch if you don't leave the house!

Knock knock.
Who's there?
Alice!
Alice who?
Alice fair in potions and spells!

Knock knock.
Who's there?
Water!
Water who?
Water you doing at the Witch's House?

Knock knock.
Who's there?
Leaf!
Leaf who?
Leaf the little Witch alone!

Knock knock.
Who's there?
Olive!
Olive who?
Olive the good Witch! She gave me yummy candy!

Knock knock.
Who's there?
Razor!
Razor who?
Razor hands if you saw the bad Witch!

Knock knock.
Who's there?
Candice!
Candice who?
Candice Witch turn my house into candy?

Knock knock.
Who's there?
Spell!
Spell who?
I'll cast a spell on you!

Knock knock.
Who's there?
Icy!
Icy who?
Icy you looking at the Witch costume!

Knock knock.
Who's there?
Alex!
Alex who?
Alex-plain how the Witch turned my friends into frogs!

Knock knock.
Who's there?
Needle!
Needle who?
Needle little help catching the Witch!

Knock knock.
Who's there?
A herd!
A herd who?
A herd the Witch would sing tonight!

Knock knock.
Who's there?
Dishes!
Dishes Who?
Dishes a very terrible Halloween Joke!

Knock knock.
Who's there?
Arfur!
Arfur who?
Arfur got how lucky I was to meet the good Witch!

Knock knock
Who's there?
Witch
Witch who?
Witch one of you took my broom?

Knock knock
Who's there
Norway
Norway who?
There's Norway the Witch left her broom behind!

Knock knock
Who's there?
Ben
Ben who?
Ben waiting for a wizard all my life

Knock knock
Who's there
Witches
Witches who?
Witches the line for trick and treat snacks?

Knock knock
Who's there
Open.
Open who?
Open the door, the Witch is angry!

Knock knock
Who's there
Andee.
Andee who?
Andee Witch just turned you into a Pumpkin!

Knock knock
Who's there
Anita.
Anita who?
Anita go home, the Witch wants to cast a spell on me!

Knock knock
Who's there
Carrie.
Carrie who?
Carrie me home, my broom overslept!

Knock knock
Who's there
Sam.
Sam who?
Sam-body poured water on the Witch!

Knock knock
Who's there
Venice.
Venice who?
Venice the Witch going to ask the wizard out for a date?

Knock knock
Who's there
Love.
Love who?
I love it when people don't know I'm a Witch

Would you rather

Would you rather…
Be a Witch who can't cast spells
or a Wizard without a wand?

Would you rather…
Be a Witch who rides a broom
or a Witch who drives a Helicopter?

Would you rather…
Be a Witch who can be melted with water
or a Witch who lives forever?

Would you rather…
Be Friends with a spooky Witch who's nice
or a beautiful Witch who's mean?

Would you rather…
eat eyeballs for breakfast
or let a Witch cast a love spell you?

Would you rather…
Be a wizard living on earth
or a Witch living in a fantasy world?

Would you rather…
Be best friends with a Witch
or a wizard?

Would you rather…
Sniff a Witch's stinky boot all day long
or eat a nasty green stew?

Would you rather…
Be an ugly Witch on Halloween
or eat coleslaw for the rest of the year?

Would you rather…
Let a Witch turn your house into candy
or chocolate?

Witchery LOL series

What did the Wizard tell the Witch?
You've got me under your spell!

What do you call a Witch who loves the beach?
Sand-Witch!

Why did the little Witch ride a bike to school?
Because her broom was broken!

Why did the Witch refuse to go to the Baseball tournament? She didn't have a bat!

Can you fly on a broom?
Yes! All it takes is some Witch-ful thinking!

What do Witches like to watch on TV?
The hex files!

Where should a 500-pound Witch go?
On a diet!

What do Witches do when it's dark?
They turn on the lights-Witch!

How do you tell twin Witches a part?
You work out which Witch is which!

Why did the Witch get a stomach-ache after eating candy?
She was goblin her candy!

What do Witches like to eat?
Ghoulash!

Why did the Witch drive to the store?
The invisible man stole her broom!

How can you differentiate between Witches?
You can't. They all have a long pointy hat!

What do you call a good Witch?
A failure!

If you want to make a Witch feel itchy and scratchy
Remove the W.

Zombies Jokes
You will laugh your head off Zombie jokes!

Zombie Puns

Q. What do vegetarian Zombies eat?
A. Grains

Q. How did the Zombie pass the test?
A. It was a no-brainer!

Q. Why are Zombies so good at playing chess?
A. Dead-ication!

Q. What did the Zombie tell the Witch?
A. Nice to eat you!

Q. Why do Zombies look different every day?
A. Because they keep losing body parts.

Q. Why shouldn't you give Zombies mashed potatoes?
A. They have already had the grave-y!

Q. Why don't humans understand Zombies?
A. Because they speak a dead language!

Q. How much does it cost to feed a Zombie?
A. An arm and a leg.

Q. What did the Zombie's mom do when she realized her son was becoming bad?
A. She grounded him!

Q. How do smart people attract Zombies?
A. They give them a piece of their minds.

Q. When you go to a birthday party for a Zombie what do you get called?
A. The life of the party!

Q. What do Zombies wear on wet days?
A. A brain coat

Q. What did the Zombie like about its prom date?
A. He appreciated her brains!

Q. What do Zombies want more than anything in the world?
A. Peace of mind!

Q. When do Zombies realize they have to go to sleep?
A. When they get dead tired!

Q. Why did the Zombie avoid swimming with sharks?
A. He got cold feet

Q. What do you call vegan Zombies?
A. Life savers!

Q. What did the Zombie say after realizing his friend wasn't honest?
A. You're dead to me!

Q. Bees that don't die are called?
A. Zombees!

Q. Why was the Zombie sent home?
A. His deodorant smelled rotten!

Q. Why did the Zombie solve the puzzle quickly?
A. It was a no-brainer!

Q. What did the Zombie tell the other Zombie who got his answers confused?
A. You're dead wrong!

Q. What can't you give a headless Zombie?
A. A headache!

Q. Why did the Zombie cross the road?
A. He was dying to get to the other side!

Q. How do polite Zombies introduce themselves?
A. I'm pleased to eat you!

Q. What do you call a Zombie with a lot of kids?
A. A mom-ster!

Q. Why was the Zombie taken to a mental hospital?
A. Because he was losing his mind!

Q. Where do Zombies swim?
A. The Dead sea!

Q. Why did the Zombie stop teaching his students?
A. He only had one pupil left!

Q. What do Zombies use to tell the future?
A. Horror-scope!

Q. How do Zombies get smart?
A. By eating lots of Smarties!

Q. What do Zombies love to eat?
A. YOU!

Q. Where do Zombies like to hang out?
A. On Dead end streets!

Q. Why do hungry Zombies like to stay in groups?
A. It's easier to grab Fast Food!

Q. Why are Zombies stupid?
A. They are Brain Dead!

Q. Why did the Zombie join the military?
A. He heard they were giving out arms!

Q. What do you call a Zombie that has children?
A. Mom-bie!

Q. Why did the Zombie join acting class?
A. He wanted to act more lively

Q. Did the Zombie finish eating the steak
A. Yes, but now he's eating his fingers!

Q. Who won the Zombie race?
A. Nobody! They are still running. Have you not seen how slow Zombies run?

Q: Why didn't the Zombie go to School Today?
A. He felt really rotten!

Q. Why are Zombies scared of crossing the road?
A. It's too early for them to cross to the other side!

Q. Why do Zombies stay in large groups?
A. Because one Zombie is a no-brainer, multiple Zombies means you run!

Q. Why are all Zombies bad?

A. Because they are all rotten people!

Q. What did the Zombie tell his human girlfriend?

A. Come over for Dinner tonight!

Q: What do you do when 50 Zombies surround your house?

A. Look at your calendar and hope that its Halloween

Knock-knock jokes

Knock knock
Who's there?
Ivana!
Ivana who?
Ivana eat your brains!

Knock knock
Who's there?
Bee.
Bee who?
Bee-ware of the Zombies approaching!

Knock knock
Who's there?
Cement.
Cement who?
Cement to scream when he saw a Zombie!

Knock knock
Who's there?
Iran
Iran who?
Iran over here because the Zombies were chasing me!

Knock knock
Who's there?
Norma
Norma who?
Norma'lly I'd go for a Witch's costume, but I'll go for a Zombie costume this time

Knock knock!
Who's there?
Zombies!
Zombies who?
Zom-bees make yummy honey, Zombies don't!

Knock knock
Who's there
Butter.
Butter who?
Butter Zombie was so polite! He wasn't going to eat us!

Knock knock
Who's there
Voodoo.
Voodoo who?
Voodoo fight a Zombie?

Knock knock
Who's there
Lettuce.
Lettuce who?
Lettuce me in there are Zombies outside!

Knock knock
Who's there
Icing
Icing who?
Icing so loud the Zombies might hear!

Knock knock.
Who's there?
Impatient Zombie!
Impatient Zombie wh?
Braaaaaainnnnsssssss

Knock knock.
Who's there?
Zeke!
Zeke who?
Zeke the Zombie and you shall find!

Knock knock.
Who's there?
Imma
Imma who?
Imma fight the Zombies till they are all gone!

Knock knock.
Who's there?
Adore!
Adore who?
Adore is between the Zombies and us, we're safe!

Knock knock.
Who's there?
Abby!
Abby who?
Abby Halloween to you!

Knock knock.
Who's there?
Isabel!
Isabel who?
Isabel ringed whenever Zombies approached us!

Knock knock.
Who's there?
Amanda!
Amanda who?
A-man-doesn't want to befriend Zombies!

Knock knock.
Who's there?
Alfie!
Alfie who?
Alfie terrible if we send the Zombies to the other side!

Knock knock.
Who's there?
Andrew!
Andrew who?
Andrew a picture of ten blood-thirsty Zombies!

Knock knock.
Who's there?
Noah!
Noah who?
Do you noah good place to hide from the Zombies?

Knock knock.
Who's there?
Zombie!
Zombie who?
A Zombie too short to ring the bell!

Knock knock.
Who's there?
Stopwatch!
Stopwatch who?
Stopwatch-a doing and close the doors before the Zombies get in the living room!

Knock knock.
Who's there?
Justin!
Justin who?
I'm Justin time to eat your Brains!

Knock knock.
Who's there?
Egg!
Egg who?
I'm eggcited to see Zombies during Halloween!

Knock knock.
Who's there?
Radio!
Radio who?
Radio not, I'm going trick or treating as a Zombie!

Knock knock.
Who's there?
Fork!
Fork who?
Fork-get it. I'm not eating brains! I'm a vegan...I eat grains!

Knock knock.
Who's there?
Java!
Java who?
Java Zombie in your room?

Knock knock.
Who's there?
Goose!
Goose who?
Goose who's knocking at your door?
Who?
Braaaaainnnnssss

Knock knock.
Who's there?
Keanu!
Keanu who?
Keanu let me in the house. A few Zombies are after me!

Knock knock.
Who's there?
Pasta!
Pasta who?
Pasta salt! This brain is too plain!

Would you rather

Would you rather ...
Be a Zombie without an eye
or a vegetarian Zombie?

Would you rather ...
Be friends with a Zombie that needs you to let him eat
a piece of your body per day
or a Zombie that doesn't do anything?

Would rather ...
Be chased by a group of Zombies
or by a group of wild monsters?

Would you rather...
Be a smelly Zombie in Halloween
or a stinky Witch?

Would you rather...
Be a Zombie during an apocalypse
or a human who survived?

Would you rather...
Be a sad Zombie with many brains to eat
or a happy Zombie with a few brains to eat?

Would you rather…
Be a Zombie who dies in the hands of human beings
or a Zombie who turns humans into Zombies?

Would you rather…
Pass all your tests
or be as stupid as Zombies?

Would you rather…
Eat brains for the rest of the year
or eat rotten pizza for the rest of the year?

Would you rather…
Live in dead-end streets where Zombies live
or in a haunted house?

Laughing Dead LOL series

Which Shampoo is a Zombies favourite?
Head and Shoulders!

Why don't Zombies like ice cream?
Because they get brain freeze!

Where do Zombies go to parties?
Club dead!

What bean is a Zombies favorite?
Human bean!

Where did the Zombie get his girlfriend from?
He dug her up!

What do you call a Zombie who dies during vacation?
Dead-ication!

Why don't Zombies eat brains with their fingers?
Because they end up eating their fingers!

Why can't a Zombie be trusted?
He keeps losing body parts!

Why do Zombies make bad comedians?
Depending on their audience they are either dying up there, or they are killing it

What happens when you tell jokes to Zombies?
They are all moans and groans.

Why did the Zombie lose the argument?
He had no leg to stand on!

What do Zombies catch during winter?
Frostbites!

What did the Zombies tell his girlfriend during Valentine's?
I want your brains, but I will settle for your heart!

What did the Zombie tell his best friend?
I like your guts!

What do Zombie in love tell each other?
I dig you!

Vampire Jokes
Fang-tastic jokes from Transylvania!

Night Walker Puns

Q. Why are Vampires a pain in the neck?
A. Because they are always in a bat mood!

Q. Why are Vampires easy to fool?
A. They are suckers!

Q. What do serious Vampires love to wear?
A. Neckties.

Q. What's a Vampire's favorite biscuit flavor?
A. Vein-illa!

Q. Which of Dracula's friends was really good at baseball?
A. The bat!

Q. Why don't Vampires wear pretty makeup?
A. Because they can't see their reflection!

Q. What did Dracula say in the line for food?
A. I'm necks please!

Q. Why was Dracula admitted to the hospital?
A. He was coffin pretty badly.

Q. After so long, why did Dracula brush his teeth?
   A. He had bat breath!

Q. Why didn't Dracula suck comedian's blood?
   A. It tastes funny!

Q. What do you call a little girl who's a Vampire?
   A. Vampirina!

Q. What is Dracula's favorite candy?
A. Suckers!

Q. What do Vampires do when they can't sleep?
A. They take a coffin break!

Q. What did Dracula's girlfriend say after she got kissed by him?
A. He really likes necking!

Q. What's it like living in Transylvania?
A. No one lives in Transylvania, Vampires are already dead

Q. What is Dracula's favorite sport?
A. Bat-Minton!

Q. What is a Vampires least favorite song?
A. "You are my sunshine!"

Q. What's a Vampires favorite mode of transport?
A. A blood vessel!

Q. When is a Vampire's favorite day of the week?
A. Fangs-day

Q. What type of dog does Dracula have?
A. A Bloodhound!

Q. Why did the police arrest the Vampire?
A. He tried to rob a blood bank!

Q. Where do Vampires eat their lunch?
A. At the casketeria!

Q. Can Vampires bite family members?
A. Only if they are blood brothers!

Q. Why didn't Dracula get married after all these years?
A. He wanted to remain a bat-chelor!

Q. Why didn't the Vampire drink his enemy's blood?
A. They have bad blood!

Q. How did the Vampire win first prize at the art competition?
A. He drew blood!

Q. Why does Dracula dislike the shower so much?
A. Because he likes the bat-tub more!

Q. What do you call a duck who has been bitten by a Vampire?
A. Count Duckula!

Q. When do Vampires see the sun?
A. Never, don't you know anything about Vampires?

Q. How did Dracula avoid paying his lunch bill?
A. He ate necks to nothing!

Q. What do little Vampires learn in school?
A. The alphabat!

Q. Where do Chinese Vampires live?
A. Fanghai!

Q. Where does each Vampire want to visit when they go to New York City?
A. They want to go to the Vampire state building!

Q. What did Dracula catch during winter?
A. He got frostbite!

Q. Where do Dracula and his family go on vacation?
A. The Isle of fright!

Q. Which tests do Vampires like?
A. Blood tests!

Q. What did the Vampire doctor say to the next patient?
A. Your necks in line!

Q. Why do Vampires come out at night?
A. To take his ghoul friend on a date!

Q. Which toothpaste do Vampires like?
A. Colgate Extreme-bite toothpaste!!

Q. Who has the scariest job in Transylvania?
A. Dentists!

Q. What should you do when you see a Vampire?
A. RUN!

Q. Why did the Vampire get fired from his Blood Bank job?
A. He got caught drinking on the job!

Q. Why doesn't Dracula work a corporate job?
A. Because he doesn't like neck-ties!

Q. Why do people like Vampires?
A. They think they are fang-tastic!

Q. What do you call it when a Vampire has housing issues?
A. A grave issue!

Q. Why doesn't Dracula get married?
A. Because there is too much at stake!

Knock-knock Jokes

Knock knock.
Who's there?
Fangs!
Fangs who?
Fangs for letting me suck your blood!

Knock knock.
Who's there?
Viper!
Viper who?
Viper your mouth, you have blood dripping!

Knock knock.
Who's there?
Getyur!
Getyur who?
Getyur fangs off my neck!

Knock knock.
Who's there?
Howie
Howie who?
Howie gonna fill the blood banks?

Knock knock.
Who's there?
Minnie!
Minnie who?
Minnie have tried to chase away Dracula but he keeps coming back!

Knock knock.
Who's there?
Alva!
Alva who?
Alva heart and don't bite my neck!

Knock knock.
Who's there?
Alfred!
Alfred who?
Alfred of the sunlight!

Knock knock.
Who's there?
Gargoyle!
Gargoyle who?
Gargoyle your mouth with garlic to keep the Vampires away!

Knock knock.
Who's there?
Chicken.
Chicken who?
Chicken the window, don't let any ray of sunlight in Dracula's house!

Knock knock.
Who's there?
Doris!
Doris who?
Doris locked and I'm trying to let Dracula out of his coffin.

Knock knock.
Who's there?
Al!
Al who?
Al suck your blood if you don't sleep early tonight!

Knock knock.
Who's there?
Curry!
Curry who?
Curry me home, I'm scared of the Vampires!

Knock knock.
Who's there?
Luke!
Luke who?
Luke through the basement, you might find some of Dracula's items!

Knock knock.
Who's there?
Tank!
Tank who?
Tank you for coming on fangsgiving day!

Knock knock.
Who's there?
Omar!
Omar who?
Omar goodness! Dracula finished all the blood in the blood banks!

Knock knock.
Who's there?
Sweden!
Sweden who?
Sweden the blood for me! I want it extra-sweet!

Knock knock.
Who's there?
Datsun!
Datsun who?
Datsun old Vampire!

Knock knock.
Who's there?
Darwin!
Darwin who?
I'll be Darwin you to visit the Vampires.

Knock knock.
Who's there?
Doris!
Doris who?
The Doris opened, you can get in Dracula's house!

Knock knock.
Who's there?
Falafel!
Falafel who?
The Vampire falafel off his bike!

Knock knock!
Who's there?
Tyson.
Tyson who?
Tyson garlic around your neck to chase away Vampires!

Knock knock
Who's there
Viper.
Viper who?
Viper the blood around your mouth!

Knock knock
Who's there
Zoom.
Zoom who?
Zoom are you calling a sucker?

Knock knock
Who's there
Vampire.
Vampire who?
I'm just writing in my Vampire diary.

Knock knock
Who's there
Wayne.
Wayne who?
Bruce Wayne, Dracula's favorite superhero.
You can call me batman.

Knock knock
Who's there
Fangs.
Fangs who?
It's fangsgiving can I join the Party?

Knock knock
Who's there
Gladys
Gladys who?
Gladys the last neck you suck today!

Knock knock
Who's there
Dracula!
Dracula who?
Count Dracula of Course!

Knock knock
Who's there
Hope.
Hope who?
Hopes the sun will set fast so I can suck your blood!

Knock knock
Who's there?
The Earl.
The Earl who?
The Early Dracula gets the best blood!

Would you rather

Would you rather...
be Dracula's dentist
or go to the dentist?

Would you rather...
be a Vampire who drinks tea instead of blood
or a Vampire who drinks blood instead of tea?

Would you rather...
live in a coffin like a Vampire
or a web like a spider?

Would you rather...
have a blood sucking bat
or snake as a pet?

Would you rather...
suck blood for the rest of your life
or eat steak?

Would you rather…
have money
or blood in your bank?

Would you rather…
be allergic to the sunshine
or allergic to garlic?

Would you rather…
live in Transylvania
or Pennsylvania?

Would you rather…
live with a group of Vampires
or live in a wild remote tribe in the middle of nowhere?

Would you rather…
be a Vampire
or a werewolf?

Frightful LOL series

What is Dracula's pet peeve?
Coffin!

How do you know a Lady Vampire likes you?
They bat their eyes at you!

What do Vampires say when they work the graveyard shift? "Have a nice bite!"

What is a Vampires car called?
A mobile blood unit!

Why was the Vampire fired from his job at the blood bank?
Because he was feeling down, so he took some B Positive.

What are a Tik-Tok Vampires followers known as?
His Fang club!

Why do you avoid making a Vampire angry?
Because he has a 'bat' temper

When do you suspect your doctor has been turned into a Vampire?
When they send you for lots of blood tests!

What do you call a cow that turns into a Vampire?
Cow-nt Dracula!

What 3 choices do you have when a Vampire chases after you?
A) Run!
B) Run!
C) Run!

What are Vampires favorite African animal?
Giraffe.

Why do Vampires Brush their teeth every day?
To get rid of bat breath!

What do you call a Vampire slayer who has eaten too many marshmallows?
Puffy the Vampire slayer!

What type of dance do Vampires enjoy?
The Fang-dango

What are women Vampires favorite shade of lipstick?
Blood Red!

Ghost Jokes
Boo-tastic Ghost jokes to spook you and your family

Q. What's a Ghost's favorite shoe?
A. Boooooots!

Q. What do you call a Ghost who writes?
A. A Ghostwriter

Q. Who did the Ghost bring to the dance?
A. His ghoul friend

Q. Where does the vegetarian Ghost get his vegetables from?
A. At the Ghostery store!

Q. What's a spirit's favorite ride?
A. A roller-Ghoster!

Q. Where do Ghosts go swimming?
A. In the Ghoul Pool!

Q. Which room in a house can a Ghost not enter?
A. Living room!

Q. What did the Ghost tell his noisy friend?
A. Spook when you're spooken to.

Q. What happened when the Ghost met his wife?
A. It was love at first fright!

Q. Which cream do Ghosts apply on their skin?
A. Vanishing cream!

Q. What do Ghosts put on their bagels?
A. Scream cheese!

Q. What are funny Ghosts called?
A. Dead funny!

Q. What does a Panda Bear Ghost eat?
A. Bam-BOO

Q. What did the girl Ghosts say when they were caught having too much fun?
A. Ghouls just wanna have fun!

Q. When do Ghosts wake up?
A. In the moaning!

Q. How do Ghosts send mail to their friends?
A. They use the Ghost office!

Q. What other places do Ghosts go swimming?
A. Lake Eerie!

Q. What can you find in a Ghost's nose?
A. Boogers!

Q. What did the vegan Ghost say to the Ghost who was eating meat?
A. I'm sorry, but I can't meet you!

Q. What trees do spirits like to stay under?
A. Ceme-trees

Q. What music do Ghosts like to play?
A. Spiritual music!

Q. What do Ghosts with poor eyesight wear?
A. A pair of Spook-tacles!

Q. Why do Ghosts hate mean people?
A. Because they lower their spirits

Q. What do Ghost use when it gets too hot?
A. The Scare-conditioner!

Q. What does a Ghost order for Dessert?
A. BOOberry Pie

Q. What is a Ghost's favorite Disney character?
A. Poca-haunt-us!

Q: What do Ghosts eat for Dinner?
A. Spook-getti

Q. How do Ghosts travel during their vacations?
A. They use Scare-planes!

Q. How can the Ghost send a letter to his family?
A. He should use a Ghost-office!

Q. Where do Ghosts refuel their cars?
A. At the ghastly station!

Q. What do baby Ghosts call their parents?
A. Transparents!

Q. What did the mommy Ghost tell the little Ghost before entering the car?
A. Don't forget to put on your sheet-belt!

Q. What do serious Ghosts wear?
A. A boo-tie!

Q. Where do famous Ghosts live in?
A. Mali-boo!

Q. Why was the Ghost scared of singing in front of the large crowd?
A. He didn't want to get booed!

Q. What do Ghosts like to do during their free time?
A. They like to watch boo-vies!

Q. What did the Ghost who's on a diet tell the waiter?
A. No scream and sugar in my coffee please!

Q. If a Ghost makes a mistake, what do you call it?
A. A booboo!

Q. Why did the Ghost go to prom?
A. To take out his boo-tiful ghoul friend!

Q. How did the little Ghost get a girlfriend?
A. He told her that she's the most boo-tiful Ghost he's ever seen!

Q. What do you call a Ghost that sits too close to the heater?
A. Toastie Ghostie!

Q. What are Ghosts' favorite smoothie?
A. Boo-berry!

Q. What game do young ghosts love to play?
A. Hide and shriek!

Q. What do Ghosts say when they are bored?
A. Booring!

Q. What happened to the actors in a haunted stage?
A. They had stage fright!

Trick or Treat Ghost Knock knock Jokes

Knock knock!
Who's there?
Ghouls.
Ghouls who?
"Ghouls just wanna have fun."

Knock knock!
Who's there?
Ghoul-deluxe.
Ghoul-deluxe who?
Ghoul-deluxe and the three scares is my favorite bedtime story!

Knock knock.
Who's there?
Howl!
Howl who?
Howl you know the Ghost was here unless you hear booooooo?

Knock knock.
Who's there?
Dishes
Dishes who?
Dishes a house haunted by scary Ghosts!

Knock knock.
Who's there?
Ivan.
Ivan who?
Ivan dress up like a Ghost for Halloween!

Knock knock.
Who's there?
Butter!
Butter who?
Butter open the door, the Ghosts are following me!

Knock knock.
Who's there?
Doughnut
Doughnut who?
Doughnut worry, it's the silly Ghost! He's harmless!

Knock knock.
Who's there?
Hugo!
Hugo who?
Hugo put your white sheets on! That way, you'll be a Ghost!

Knock knock.
Who's there?
Harry!
Harry who?
Harry up! The spirits are leaving the cemetery!

Knock knock.
Who's there?
Imogen!
Imogen who?
Imogen living with spooky Ghosts!

Knock knock.
Who's there?
Deesa
Deesa who?
Deesapear before the scary Ghost sees you!

Knock knock.
Who's there?
Mikey
Mikey who?
Mi-key to the haunted house doesn't fit in the keyhole!

Knock knock.
Who's there?
Juicer
Juicer who?
Ju-serve the Ghost some tea!

Knock knock.
Who's there?
Ghost!
Ghost who?
Gho-start the show before the crowd starts booing!

Knock knock.
Who's there?
Ida!
Ida who?
I dumped the Ghost's sheets in the washing machine.

Knock knock.
Who's there?
Hideout!
Hideout who?
Hideout you'll see the Ghost!

Knock knock.
Who's there?
Ivory!
Ivory who?
Ivory turned the Ghost to the cemetery.

Knock knock.
Who's there?
Exercise!
Exercise who?
Exercise a lot if you want to chase the Ghosts away!

Knock knock.
Who's there?
Jubilee!
Jubilee who?
Ju believe me if I told you this house is haunted?

Knock knock.
Who's there?
Jano!
Jano who?
Jano-tice how easy it is to spot Ghosts during Halloween?

Knock knock.
Who's there?
Justice!
Justice who?
Justice once can we go out Ghost haunting?

Knock knock.
Who's there?
Shelia!
Shelia who?
She loves her Ghost boyfriend!

Knock knock.
Who's there?
Winner!
Winner who?
Winner you going to stop chasing the spirits?

Knock knock!
Who's there?
Ghost.
Ghost who?
Gho-stand there, I'll bring you the best Halloween costume!

Knock knock!
Who's there?
Bean.
Bean who?
Bean waiting to scare the kids during Halloween!

Knock knock!
Who's there?
Boo!
Boo who?
Boo-hoo don't be scared. I'm not a Ghost!

Knock knock!
Who's there?
Justin.
Justin who?
Justin time for Halloween!

Knock knock
Who's there
Orange?
Orange who?
Orange you happy I didn't say Boo?

Knock knock
Who's there
Dana.
Dana who?
I Dana know where Cassper is!

Knock knock
Who's there
Candy
Candy who?
Candy dog stop chasing the Ghost away!

Knock knock
Who's there
Sheet?
Sheet who?
Please put your sheet-belts on!

Would you rather

Would you rather…
live with Ghosts of old pirates in a large ship
or Ghost of old mermaids?

Would you rather…
be a Ghost who doesn't say "boo!"
or a spirit who lives in the living room?

Would you rather…
live with Ghosts
or live on mars?

Would you rather…
be friends with a Ghost who you can't see
or be enemies with a Ghost you can see?

Would you rather…
be a Ghostbuster
or an exorcist?

Would you rather…
see Ghosts in real life
or be a normal kid with a normal boring life?

Would you rather…
be a Ghost's pet
or pet a Ghost?

Would you rather be…
a scared Ghost
or a brave human being?

Would you rather…
be a Ghost who can't pass through walls
or a Ghost who lives alone?

Would you rather…
get lost in a haunted house
or a Witch's house?

Would you rather…
be a Ghost who lives in the sea
or a Ghost who lives in an abandoned church?

Spirited LOL series!

Where do classy Ghosts shop for their outfits?
Boo-tiques!

What did the Ghost tell his ghoul friend?
Get a life!

What happened to the spirit who gave a dull performance!
It was booed off the stage

Who makes the best cheerleaders?
Ghosts, because they have team spirit!

Why was the Ghost angry at the Witch for casting a rain spell?
Because it dampened his spirit!

What do you call it when a group of Ghosts robs a bank?
A polterheist

How do Ghosts begin their letters?
Tomb whom it may concern!

How did the little Ghost pass his exam?
By going through his paper over and over again!

Why do Mom Ghost not like sending their Ghost kids out of the house?
Because Ghosts are always mist when outside!

What do you call the Ghost who is a soccer goalkeeper?
A Ghoulie!

Where do many Ghosts live?
South Scarealina!

Why do Ghosts moan in winter?
because it's cold under their sheets!

What do Ghosts use to wash their Ghost hair?
They use sham-booo!

What is a Ghosts favorite play?
Romeo and Ghouliette!

What do Italian Ghosts love to eat?
spook-hetti bolognaise

Halloween Jokes

Amazingly bad Halloween jokes to make you and your family chuckle!

Pumpkin Spice Puns

Q. Why did the dog chase the skeleton?
A. He had a bone to chew with him!

Q. When do monsters cook their victims?
A. Fry-day!

Q. Why didn't the skeleton skydive?
A. He didn't have any guts!

Q. Why was the scarecrow promoted?
A. Because he was head and shoulders above the rest!

Q. Why didn't the skeleton go out trick or treating?
A. Because he had nobody to go out with.

Q. What do monsters love to eat during Halloween?
A. Ice scream!

Q. What do you call a skeleton who doesn't like to work?
A. A lazy bone!

Q. What did the spider say when he was caught lying?
A. I'm in a web of lies!

Q. Why did the skeleton go to the butchery?
A. To get a spare rib!

Q. What would you call a monster that doesn't have a neck?
A. The Lack-neck monster.

Q. Why don't skeletons get angry?
A. Nothing gets under their skin!

Q. What did the werewolf tell the barber?
A. I need a haircut!

Q. What did the scarecrow say when he was electrocuted
A. I'm shocked!

Q. What did the monster say after she applied makeup?
A. Eye-lashed out!

Q. What do owls say during Halloween?
A. Happy Owl-ween!

Q. Where did the skeleton find his new friend?
A. He dug him up!

Q. Why didn't the mummy see who stole all the trick or treat candy?
A. He was too wrapped up in his problems to notice!

Q. What do Ghosts like to eat for dinner?
A. Boo-lgonie sandwiches!

Q. What sound does the Zombie T-rex make when he sleeps?
A. Dina-snore!

Q. Where do werewolves store their stuff?
A. In the were-house!

Q. If there was a musical instrument the skeleton would play, that would be?
A. Trom-bone!

Q. Which city do Werewolves live in?
A. Howly-wood!

Q. What did the mummy tell the woman who kept talking?
A. Let's wrap this up!

Q. Why was the Skeleton laughing all the time?
A. He kept hitting his funny bone!

Q. Why did the police arrest the Skeleton?
A. He was bad to the bone!

Q. Why did the Skeleton confront Dracula?
A. He had a bone to pick with him!

Q. Why do spirits hang out with ghouls?
A. Because spirits are a ghoul's best friend!

Q. What did the dog tell the skeleton?
A. woof, woof, woof...which in human is 'I dig you!'

Q. What does bigfoot say when he goes out trick or treating?
A. Trick or Feet?

Q. What cookies do spirits like?
A. Ghoul Scout cookies!

Q. When do Goblins eat all their food?
A. Chewsday!

Q. Why didn't the monster score the goal?
A. The ghoul keeper caught the ball!

Q. How do monsters like their kids?
A. Terri-fried!

Q. What do you call a Witch who adds potions to coco pops?
A. Cereal Killer!

Q. What did the monster say about the invisible man's costume?
A. I love how see-through your costume is!

Q. What do married pumpkins call each other?
A. "Hey, Pumpkin?"

Q. Why do Ghosts like Black Friday?
A. Because they are Bargain Haunters

Q. What do you call a black cat whose had a lot of lemons for dinner?
A. Sour-puss!

Q. Why did the headless man study so hard?
A. He wanted to get ahead in life!

Q. Why did the Zombie put lipstick on its head?
A. He was told to make up his mind!

Q. How do you chase away demons?
A. By exorcising!

Q. What do you call a Pumpkin with an eye covering
A. Pumpkin Patch!

Q. Who is a werewolf's cousin?
A. A Whatwolf!

Q. What happens if you make a cannibal angry?
A. You'd get in hot water!

Q. What do you call a werewolf who likes to dress up?
A. Wearwolf!

Knock-knock jokes

Knock knock.
Who's there?
Candy!
Candy who?
Candy boy give me a few popsicles?

Knock knock.
Who's there?
Armageddon!
Armageddon who?
This place is too spooky! Armageddon out of here!

Knock knock.
Who's there?
Ice cream!
Ice cream who?
Ice scream every time I hear the wolves howl!

Knock knock.
Who's there?
Ben!
Ben who?
Ben waiting to trick or treat with my friends!

Knock knock.
Who's there?
Howl!
Howl who?
Howl you know the Ghost was here unless you hear booooooo

Knock knock.
Who's there?
Egypt!
Egypt who?
Egypt you who saw the mummy?

Knock knock.
Who's there?
Gladys
Gladys who?
Gladys time to go trick or treating!

Knock knock.
Who's there?
Orange!
Orange who?
Orange you glad you saw the skeleton?

Knock knock.
Who's there?
Wooden shoe.
Wooden shoe who?
Wooden shoe want to see huge spiders?

Knock knock.
Who's there?
Canoe!
Canoe who?
Canoe go on a boat ride to see the Loch Ness monster with me?

Knock knock.
Who's there?
Hans!
Hans who?
Hans off the candy! It's for trick or treating!

Knock knock.
Who's there?
Peas!
Peas who?
Peas let the ghouls pass!

Knock knock.
Who's there?
Howl!
Howl who?
Happy howl-o-ween!

Knock knock.
Who's there?
Ooze!
Ooze who?
Ooze werewolf went out last night?

Knock knock.
Who's there?
Abbott!
Abbot who?
Abbott time we get to eat yummy Halloween candy!

Knock knock.
Who's there?
Essen!
Essen who?
Essen it fun to go out during Halloween?

Knock knock.
Who's there?
Police!
Police who?
Police give the skeleton some space!

Knock knock.
Who's there?
Emma!
Emma who?
Emma leave some pumpkins for you to carve!

Knock knock.
Who's there?
Max!
Max who?
Max no difference whether you're a werewolf or a fox during Halloween!

Knock knock.
Who's there?
Bone!
Bone who?
Bone petite! It's time to eat yummy spookhetti!

Knock knock.
Who's there?
Eddie!
Eddie who?
Eddie time to see mummies in the museum.

Knock knock!
Who's there?
Albert Einstein's cousin
Who?
Frank Einstein!

Knock knock!
Who's there?
Were.
Were who?
The werewolves are coming...run!!!!!

Knock knock!
Who's there?
Wine.
Wine who?
Wine are you laughing at these Halloween jokes?

Knock knock!
Who's there?
Abbott.
Abbott who?
Abbott the mission! The monsters are real!

Knock, Knock!!
Who's there?
Twick.
Twick who?
Twick or Tweet!

Knock, Knock!!
Who's there?
Dustin !
Dustin who?
Dustin off last year's Halloween Costume for you!

Knock knock!
Who's there?
Police.
Police who?
Police stay with me during Halloween, I'm scared!

Knock knock
Who's there?
Fozzie
Fozzie who?
Fozzie third time, let's go trick or treating!

Knock knock
Who's there?
Bone!
Bone who!
Bone appetite. It's time to eat some ribs!

Knock knock
Who's there?
Emma.
Emma who?
Emma go to the other town during Halloween!

Would you rather

Would you rather…
have the coolest Halloween costume yet no one
knows it was you
or the lamest Halloween costume yet everyone knows
it was you?

Would you rather…
eat all your candy during Halloween
or keep some for the next day?

Would you rather…
hear werewolves howl during Halloween
or be chased by a group of mummies?

Would you rather…
turn into a real monster during Halloween
or just wear a regular Halloween costume?

Would you rather…
be friends with an angry zoo lion
or a cheerful tiger?

Would you rather…
be Batman
or Superman during Halloween?

Would you rather…
eat all your friend's Halloween candy
or share it evenly amongst your friends?

Would you rather…
carve pumpkins during Halloween
or make everyone's costume?

Would you rather…
meet an alien's spaceship during Halloween
or meet a group of spirits in the cemetery?

Would you rather…
see a dog chase a skeleton
or a Ghost chase you?

Happy Halloween LOL Series!

What do ghosts tell around the Camp Fire?
Scary Human Stories

What do you do if a Zombie Teen girl rolls her eye at you?
Roll them back to her!

What do you call a Zombie Comedian?
Dead Funny!

Why are Ghosts good builders?
Because they use a Spirit Level!

How did the Skeleton pass his exams?
He boned up the answers!

Why was the child wrapping himself with bandages?
He was just imitating her mummy!

Who won the skeleton beauty contest?
No body!

Why do Mummies not have friends?
because they're too wrapped up in themselves!

Why are Ghosts bad at telling Lies?
Because you can see right through them!

What do you call a Pumpkin Comedian?
A joke-o'-lantern!

What do you call a Fat pumpkin?
Plumpkins!

What does a Ghoul call its parents?
Deady and Mummy!

Why don't skeletons hug?
They can't make body contact

Why don't mummies relax?
They don't want to unwind!

How can you hide a mummy?
By using masking tape!

Why are Halloween Monsters so strong?
Because they have been Pumpkin-Iron

Conclusion

Our mission at Konnectd Kids is to ensure you and your family have a fun filled Halloween with fun experiences that turn into remarkable memories!

Our Trick or Treat: Silly Halloween Jokes for Kids book was made specifically for Halloween and the humor and fun that this time of year lends itself. We truly hope that you and your family will enjoy this great book and invite you to take a look at some of our other Halloween themed books.

Have a Happy Halloween.

My final request…

Being a smaller author, reviews help me tremendously!

It would mean the world to me if you could leave a review by going to the link below.

If you or your kids enjoyed these Halloween jokes then please go to this link that will take you to Amazon to leave a review

www.konnectdkids.com/review

It only takes 30 seconds but means so much to me!

Thank you and I can't wait to see your thoughts.

Vampires Coloring Book	QR	https://tinyurl.com/y26ymmqy
Witches Coloring Book	QR	https://tinyurl.com/y2z39oow
Zombie Coloring Book	QR	https://tinyurl.com/y2uzcpl4
Halloween Coloring Book	QR	https://tinyurl.com/y4scbln5

More Konnectd Kids Books available on Amazon:
www.konnectdkids.com/books

Visit us at:
www.konnectdkids.com

Our Books and Products:
www.konnectdkids.com/books
www.konnectdsupply.com
www.etsy.com/shop/konnectd
konnectd.redbubble.com

Find us on Instagram
@Konnectdkids

Follow us on Facebook
facebook.com/Konnectdkids

Join our Facebook Group
(Free Books and giveaways)
https://www.facebook.com/groups/konnectdkidsgroup

Join our Halloween Facebook Group
https://www.facebook.com/groups/halloweenjam

Made in the USA
Columbia, SC
18 October 2020